THE EARTH IN SPACE

Peter Riley

W

FRANKLIN WATTS
LONDON•SYDNEY

First published in 1998 by
Franklin Watts
96 Leonard Street, London
EC2A 4RH

Franklin Watts Australia
14 Mars Road
Lane Cove
NSW 2066

© Franklin Watts 1998

Editor: Sarah Snashall
Art director: Robert Walster
Designer: Mo Choy
Picture research: Sue Mennell

Artwork: Sebastian
Quigley/Linden Artists and
Peter Bull

A CIP catalogue record for
this book is available from
the British Library.

ISBN 0 7496 2964 9

Dewey classification 525

Printed in Belgium

Picture credits: AKG Photo,
London p. 28t; Bruce Coleman
pp. cover, 11t; Genesis Space
Photo Library pp. 10b (NASA),
11b (NASA); Robert Harding
p. 26t; Image Bank p. 17 (Simon
Wilkinson); NASA p. 20b;
Planet Earth Pictures pp. 5t, 12t,
28b; Popperfoto p. 27
(JPL/Reuters); Rex Features pp.
22 (Chine Nouvelle), 26b; Science
Photo Library pp. 6 (Royal
Observatory, Edinburgh/AAIB),
8t (NASA), 12b (NASA), 16
(NASA), 20t (David Nunuk), 23
(Pekka Parvianen), 24t (NASA),
24b (Pekka Parvianen), 25t (Frank
Zullo), 25b (John Sanford), 29
(NASA); pp14–15m; Stock Market
pp. 4 top, 18, 19, 14–15 (Tom V.
Sant/Geosphere Project);
Telegraph Colour Library p. 10t

CONTENTS

WHAT IS SPACE?

When you look up into the night sky, you are looking out into space. It begins about 1,000 kilometres above your head, but nobody knows where it ends. The Sun, stars and planets including the Earth are all in space.

As you look up into the night sky, the clouds are in the atmosphere. The Moon, the planet Venus and the stars are in space.

THE ATMOSPHERE AND SPACE

The air we breathe is part of the atmosphere. The atmosphere is a mixture of gases which forms a layer over the surface of the Earth. The Earth's gravity pulls the gases towards the planet. About 1,000 kilometres above the Earth, the force of gravity becomes too weak to pull the gases. This is where the atmosphere ends and space begins. In space, it is dark and cold. There is no air, but there are clouds of gas and dust.

The Sun

THE BIG BANG

Many scientists believe that about 15,000 million years ago there was a huge explosion called the Big Bang. After the Big Bang the universe formed. Most of the universe is made up of dark empty space, but it also contains billions of stars. The Big Bang began at a small point like the dot on this 'i', after which the universe expanded in all directions. It is still expanding today.

This photograph is a very deep view of space. It shows hundreds of galaxies. The blue galaxies are new and the red galaxies are old. The bright light in the middle is a star.

GRAVITY AND THE STARS

A force called gravity acts between objects in space. It pulls them together or makes them move round each other. It pulls particles of matter together to make stars. The stars form in groups called galaxies. There may be hundreds of millions of stars in a galaxy and there are thousands of millions of galaxies in the universe. The Sun and the Earth are in the Milky Way Galaxy.

The Milky Way Galaxy has a spiral shape.

Stars

M ost of the lights we see in the sky are stars. A star is a huge ball of gas that is constantly changing and turning, giving out heat and light.

A star is formed when gases in a huge gas cloud, called a nebula, are pulled together by gravity.

WHY STARS SHINE

A star is made from two gases. They are called hydrogen and helium. At the centre of a star, the force of gravity is so great that it pushes hydrogen atoms together to form helium atoms. As this change takes place, large amounts of energy are released. They pass through the star and escape from its surface as light and heat.

WHEN STARS DIE

Stars do not last forever. Eventually they run out of hydrogen. When a yellow star dies, it swells into a large red star and then shrinks to form a white dwarf star which eventually stops shining.

Large stars collapse as their hydrogen store runs out. If the star collapses very quickly, it explodes and forms a super nova. The exploding star gives out huge amounts of light and dust. The force of gravity of the remaining material at the centre of a super nova may be so strong that not even light can escape from its surface, and a black hole forms.

When a yellow star runs out of hydrogen it swells up and cools down.

The constellation of the Great Bear can be seen in the northern hemisphere.

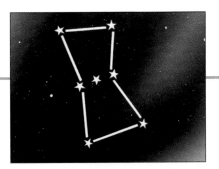

The constellation of Orion can be seen in both hemispheres.

The Southern Cross can be seen in the southern hemisphere.

CONSTELLATIONS

Almost all the stars we see in the night sky are in the Milky Way Galaxy. They are really at different distances from the Earth, but they seem to be grouped together. These groups are called constellations. Each one is named after the shape it makes in the sky. The people who named them lived long ago and named them after objects, animals and gods.

INVESTIGATE!

Look for constellations in the night sky. Start by using one of the constellations in the picture. Are all the stars in a constellation the same brightness? Are they the same colour?

As it cools, it changes colour to red. The large red star is known as a red giant.

Later the star shrinks and loses gas and dust into space. It becomes a white dwarf star.

Eventually the star stops giving out light. When this happens the star becomes a black dwarf star.

THE SOLAR SYSTEM

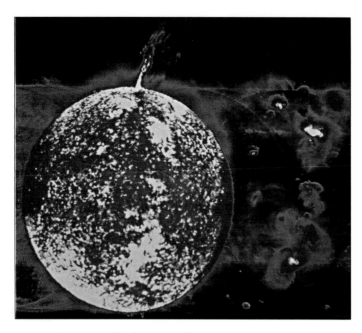

Jets of gas called solar flares shoot out from the Sun's surface.

The Sun that we see in the sky is a star. It did not form at the beginning of the universe. It formed from a cloud of gas and dust made by other stars. This cloud also formed the other objects around the Sun. We call the Sun and the objects around it, the Solar System.

HOW THE SOLAR SYSTEM FORMED

About 5,000 million years ago there was a cloud of gas and dust in the Milky Way Galaxy that was about 1.5 million million kilometres across. A star exploded nearby and sent shock waves rushing through the cloud. The shock waves pushed on the cloud and made it turn round and round and form a disc. The gases and dust inside the disc swirled round its centre. Most of the hydrogen and helium collected at the centre of the disc and formed the Sun – a yellow star.

Neptune

■ INVESTIGATE!

Stars twinkle, but planets shine. Look for a planet in the sky and see it change position every night.

THE PLANETS

Most of the remaining gases and dust formed spinning spheres
of matter called the planets. One of these planets is the Earth.
Each planet travels in a path around the Sun called an orbit.
Between the orbits of Mars and Jupiter a band
of rocks called asteroids formed
into a belt around
the Sun.

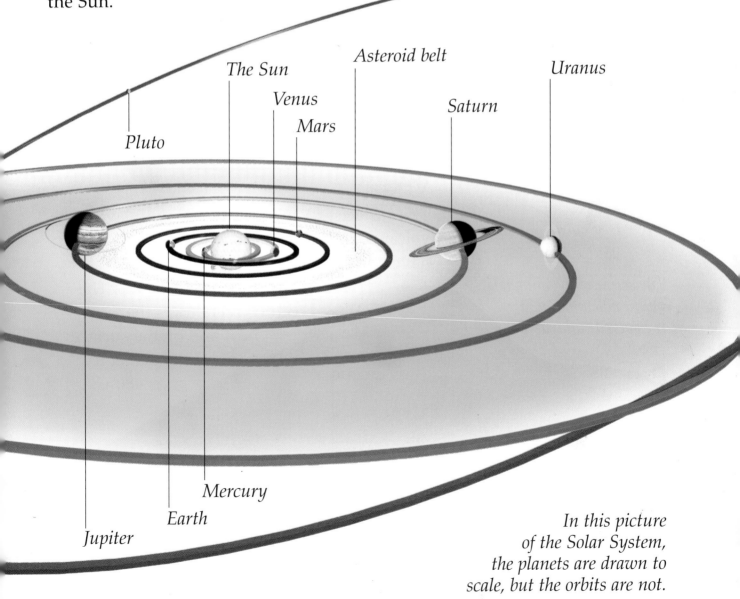

Pluto

The Sun

Venus

Mars

Asteroid belt

Saturn

Uranus

Mercury

Earth

Jupiter

*In this picture
of the Solar System,
the planets are drawn to
scale, but the orbits are not.*

THE INNER PLANETS

The surface of Mercury is covered in craters.

The planets in the Solar System can be divided into two groups – the inner planets and the outer planets. The orbits of the inner planets are inside the asteroid belt. All the inner planets are made of rock.

MERCURY

Mercury is the closest planet to the Sun. It has a rocky surface and no atmosphere to trap heat. It rotates very slowly. One side faces the Sun for about 29 Earth days and heats up to a temperature of 430°C. On the side facing away from the Sun the temperature drops to –185°C.

VENUS

The surface of Venus is covered with lava from volcanoes. The atmosphere is full of gases which have also escaped from volcanoes. The gases form thick orange clouds. This atmosphere traps the Sun's heat and on the surface of the planet it is 480°C.

The surface of Venus has many volcanoes and is covered in lava.

EARTH

Most of the Earth is covered with water. The atmosphere around it is a mixture of mainly two gases, nitrogen and oxygen. The amount of heat reaching the Earth from the Sun is sufficient to keep it warm enough for living things to survive.

The Earth has large amounts of water. This has allowed life to develop.

MARS

The surface of Mars is covered in red rocks and dust. It may reach 15°C when the Sun shines on it, but the average temperature at its equator is –50°C. It has is a thin atmosphere which contains carbon dioxide. Winds blow the dust into huge clouds. There are canyons and dried-up river beds on Mars which suggest that once the planet had water running over its surface.

Mars is red because it is covered in iron oxide – a substance commonly known as rust!

THE OUTER PLANETS

Four of the outer planets are huge and made mostly from gases and liquids. The outermost planet is much smaller and is made out of rock.

SATURN

Like Jupiter, Uranus and Neptune, Saturn has an atmosphere of hydrogen, helium and methane. Its surface is an ocean of liquid hydrogen and helium. The temperature of the high clouds in its atmosphere is –180°C. Saturn is surrounded by large rings.

The rings of Saturn are made from of ice, rock and dust which orbit the planet.

JUPITER

Jupiter is the largest planet. It is covered in thick high clouds and has 16 moons. The fast turning speed of the planet sweeps the atmosphere into bands across its surface. Below the clouds is a vast ocean of liquid hydrogen.

The giant red spot is a hurricane which is bigger than the Earth. One of Jupiter's moons can also be seen in this photograph.

URANUS

The axis of Uranus is tilted over making the planet spin on its side. Around Uranus there are small rings of black rocks and dust. The temperature of the high clouds in the atmosphere is –216°C. Beneath them is an ocean of water, liquid methane and ammonia.

Uranus and Neptune are blue due to methane in their atmospheres.

NEPTUNE

Neptune has a number of small rings like those of Uranus. The temperature of the high clouds in the atmosphere is –214°C. The winds on Neptune are the strongest in the Solar System. The gases in the atmosphere move at speeds up to 2,200 kilometres per hour. Below the atmosphere is an ocean of water, liquid methane and ammonia.

PLUTO

Pluto is a small rocky planet with a surface temperature of –230°C. Scientists are not sure of the conditions there but it is thought the surface is covered with ice and frozen gases.

Pluto has a moon called Charon which is almost half the size of Pluto.

INVESTIGATE!

Put a globe next to a table lamp and turn it to show how night and day occur. Tilt the globe so the axis is at 97° like the axis of Uranus. How does the tilt affect the night and day on Uranus?

THE MOVING EARTH

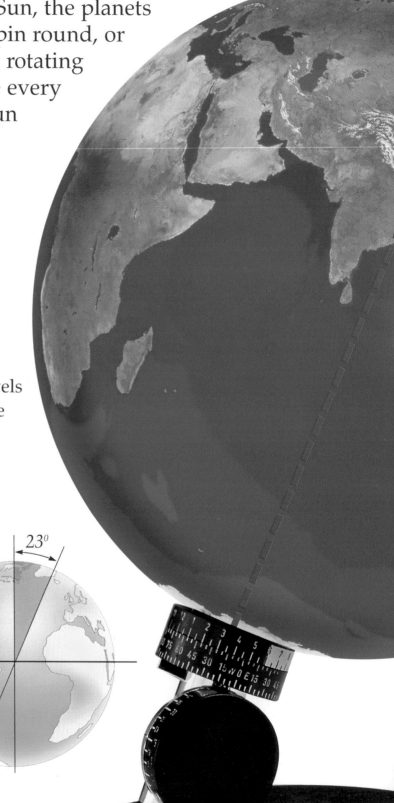

As well as orbiting the Sun, the planets in the Solar System spin round, or rotate. Jupiter is the fastest rotating planet. It spins round once every 9 hours 50 minutes. The Sun also spins, taking 24 days to spin round once.

THE TILT OF THE EARTH

The Earth rotates once every 24 hours. It rotates on its axis. The axis runs through the centre of the Earth between the North Pole and the South Pole.

The level at which the Earth travels around the Sun is called its plane of orbit. The axis of the Earth is tilted at an angle to this plane. The Earth remains tilted at the same angle and pointing in the same direction as it moves round in its orbit.

23^0

Plane of orbit

The angle of tilt is measured from a line which is at right angles to the plane of orbit.

Axis

MOVING IN ORBIT

All the planets are held in their orbits by forces of gravity. These pulling forces act between the Sun and the planets and between the planets themselves.

The orbit is in the form of an oval, or ellipse. This means that there are two places in the orbit of a planet where it is closest to the Sun and two places where it is furthest away.

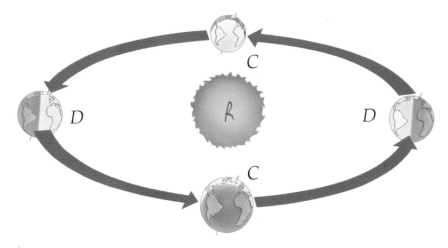

The position of the Earth in four places in its orbit. The closest points to the Sun are marked with C and the most distant points are marked with a D.

Globes are always mounted to show the tilt of the Earth in its orbit.

INVESTIGATE!

Ask an adult to attach some string to a table tennis ball. Go outside and swing the ball around your hand. Pretend your hand is the Sun, the ball is the Earth and the string is the gravity between them. Find out what would happen if there were no gravity by letting go of the string.

THE EARTH AND SUNLIGHT

Only the half of the Earth facing the Sun is lit by sunlight. When one half of the Earth has sunlight, the other is in darkness. As the Earth rotates, almost every place on the planet has a period of day-time and a period of night-time.

In this photograph, half the Earth and half the Moon are lit by sunlight.

SUMMER AND WINTER

As the Earth moves in its orbit there is a time when the North Pole is tilted towards the Sun and the South Pole is tilted away from the Sun. When this happens, places close to the North Pole have 24 hours of sunlight and other places in the northern hemisphere have days with more hours of sunlight than hours of darkness.

A

When the Earth is at A, it is summer in the northern hemisphere.

At the same time, places close to the South Pole have 24 hours of darkness and other places in the southern hemisphere have more hours of darkness than of sunlight. It is summer in the northern hemisphere and winter in the southern hemisphere.

Set up a globe next to a table lamp. Look down on the globe and turn it anti-clockwise. Find your country on the globe. See where it is dark when your country is in the light.

When the Earth is at B, it is summer in the southern hemisphere.

As the Earth moves round in its orbit, the North Pole gradually comes to point away from the Sun and the South Pole gradually comes to point towards it. This change makes the day time shorter in the northern hemisphere and longer in the southern hemisphere. When this happens it is summer in the southern hemisphere and winter in the northern hemisphere.

The equator is always pointing towards the Sun. The length of day does not change here, and the weather does not get hotter or colder, but stays very hot.

17

THE SUN IN THE SKY

When the day begins, the Sun rises over the eastern horizon. During the day, the Sun moves across the sky until it sinks beneath the western horizon. In all this time, the Sun has not really moved in space. It is the rotating Earth that makes the Sun appear to move.

THE RISING AND SINKING SUN

At any one place on Earth, the Sun rises in the sky in the morning because the place is turning towards the Sun. At midday, the place is facing the Sun directly and the Sun appears to be overhead. From midday until sunset, the place is turning away from the Sun and the Sun appears to sink in the sky.

In the morning the Sun appears above the horizon.

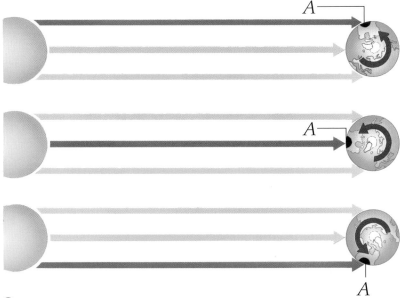

From A, the Sun can just be seen over the eastern horizon.

The Earth has turned and now from A, the Sun is seen directly overhead.

The Earth has turned further and the Sun now seems to be sinking below the western horizon.

SHADOWS AND TIME

As sunlight shines on objects on the ground, the objects cast shadows. At the beginning of the morning, the shadows are long and point towards the west. During the morning, as the Sun rises, the shadows become shorter and point towards the north in the northern hemisphere and towards the south in the southern hemisphere. In the afternoon, as the Sun sinks, the shadows become longer again and point towards the east. The position of the Sun and shadows have been used for thousands of years to measure time.

The time of day can be told from a sundial by looking at the position of the shadow.

■ INVESTIGATE!

Find the east and west horizons by watching the Sun rise and set. Work out the direction of north and south.

THE MOON

A t night when the Sun has gone down, the Moon glows in the sky. The Moon is the Earth's natural satellite. It orbits the Earth while the Earth orbits the Sun.

WHAT IS A MOON?

A moon is an object made of rock that moves in an orbit around a planet. It may be spherical like the Earth's Moon or have a more irregular shape like the two moons of Mars.

The Moon does not create its own light – it reflects light from the Sun.

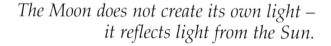

THE TURNING MOON

The Moon is only about a quarter of the Earth's size. It orbits the Earth at a distance of only 384,622 kilometres from the Earth. It takes 29.5 days to travel around the Earth once.

The Moon rotates slowly as it moves in its orbit. It rotates with the same speed as it orbits the Earth. This means that it always keeps the same side facing the Earth.

The Moon's surface is covered in mountains which appear white and dusty plains which appear grey.

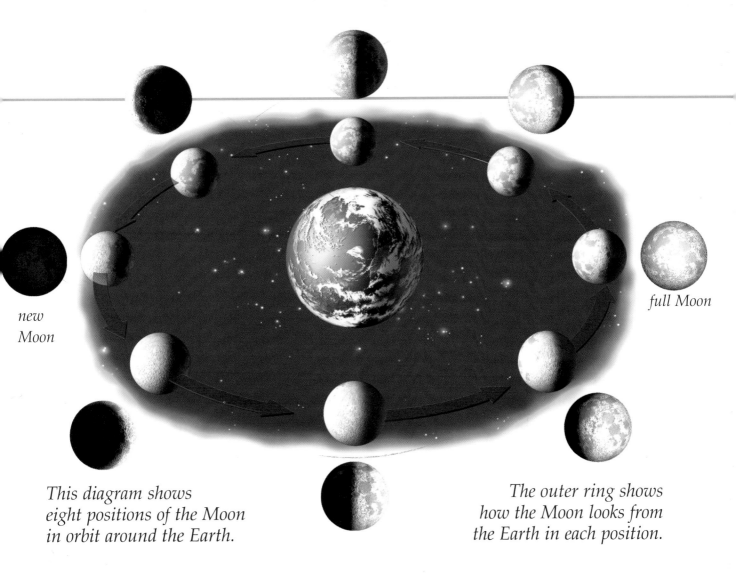

new Moon

full Moon

This diagram shows
eight positions of the Moon
in orbit around the Earth.

The outer ring shows
how the Moon looks from
the Earth in each position.

THE PHASES OF THE MOON

The amount of the Moon that is lit up in the sky
depends on its position in orbit. One side of the
Moon is always fully lit but it is not always the
side facing the Earth. If the side that is fully lit is
facing away from us, our side of the Moon is
dark. As the Moon moves in its orbit, we can see
more of its fully-lit side. First we see just a small
part of it and the Moon is called a new Moon.
Eventually the whole of the fully-lit side is facing
the Earth. This is called a full Moon.

These changes in the Moon are called the phases
of the Moon.

INVESTIGATE!

Try to draw the
Moon every night
for a month and
compare your
pictures with the
phases of the Moon
on this page.

ECLIPSES

O nce every orbit, the Moon is the same side of the
Earth as the Sun. When this happens, we do not
see the Moon because our side of the Moon is dark and
the Sun is bright in the sky. The Moon is also usually in
a different part of the sky from the Sun. If it was in the
same part of the sky, it would cover up the Sun's light.

AN ECLIPSE OF THE SUN

Sometimes the Sun, the Moon and the Earth do line up. If this
happens when the Moon and the Sun are in the sky at the same time,
the Moon comes between the Earth and the Sun. This is called a solar
eclipse because the light of the Sun is eclipsed, or covered up.

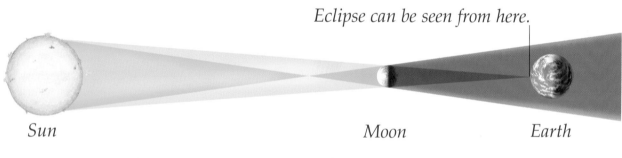

Eclipse can be seen from here.

Sun   *Moon*   *Earth*

*During a
solar eclipse,
the dark
Moon moves
in front of
the Sun.*

AN ECLIPSE OF THE MOON

Sometimes the Sun, the Earth and the Moon line up with the Earth in the middle. When this happens, the Earth stops the light of the Sun from reaching the Moon. Without the light of the Sun, the Moon stops glowing.

This is called a lunar eclipse because the Moon appears to have been covered up. During a lunar eclipse, the shadow of the Earth passes across the Moon until the Moon is covered up.

The Moon moves into the shadow of the Earth during an eclipse of the Moon.

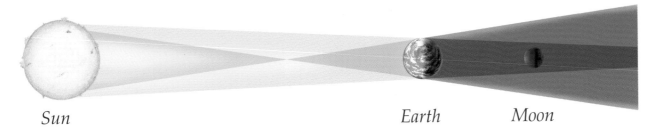

Sun   *Earth*   *Moon*

During a lunar eclipse, the light of the Sun cannot reach the Moon and make it shine.

INVESTIGATE!

Use a globe, a tennis ball and a torch to show the eclipse of the Sun and the Moon. For the eclipse of the Sun, move the tennis ball between the globe and the torch. For the eclipse of the Moon, move the globe between the tennis ball and the torch.

SPACE RUBBLE

The asteroid Ida which has its own tiny moon.

After the Sun and the planets formed, there were many pieces of rock, icy chunks of frozen gases and particles of dust that remained moving through space. They formed smaller objects in the Solar System than the Sun and planets.

ASTEROIDS

Asteroids are lumps of rock that move in orbit around the Sun. Most of the asteroids move in orbit at a distance of 300–500 million kilometres from the Sun. They form a ring called the asteroid belt. Some asteroids are hundreds of kilometers across. Others are the size of a grain of sand.

COMETS

A comet is a huge lump of ice and rock which moves in an orbit around the Sun. Billions of tiny particles leave the Sun every second and move through space. They form the solar wind. When a comet comes near to the Sun, the particles in the solar wind push against the comet and a tail of gas and a tail of dust is produced.

Comet Hale-Bopp, a very bright comet, was seen from 1995–97.

METEORS

Meteors are small pieces of rock like pebbles, or the dust from the tails of comets. As the Earth moves along its orbit, these space rocks and dust are swept into the atmosphere.

The meteors rub against the gases in the atmosphere. This makes them heat up so much that they make a streak of light in the sky as they burn away. Another name for a meteor is a shooting star.

Here, a streak of light made by a meteor can be seen in the sky.

METEORITES

Meteorites are larger pieces of rock than meteors. They do not burn up when they enter the Earth's atmosphere but fall to the ground. If a meteor is large it makes a crater on the Earth's surface.

This meteorite crater in Arizona, USA, is 800 metres wide.

INVESTIGATE!

Drop small stones into sand from different heights and compare the craters they make.

INVESTIGATING SPACE

There are many ways of investigating space.

TELESCOPES

Telescopes provide a way of looking at things that are very far away. Some telescopes collect light rays from space, others collect radio waves. Most telescopes are on Earth, but there are also telescopes in orbit around the Earth. The telescopes in orbit can collect light and radio waves from deep space.

The Hubble Space Telescope which has sent back to Earth many of the pictures that appear in this book.

SPACECRAFT

A spacecraft carries scientific equipment or astronauts into space. It has to travel very fast to break free from the pull of the Earth's gravity and enter space.

When spacecraft reach space, they usually move in orbit around the Earth. Some spacecraft are designed to move out of orbit and explore other places in space.

The rockets move the spacecraft away from the Earth at great speed.

This robot vehicle was used to investigate the surface of Mars.

SPACE PROBES

A space probe is a spacecraft which carries cameras and scientific equipment such as thermometers. It may also carry robot vehicles to explore the surface of other planets. The space probe sends the information it collects back to a space centre on Earth.

When a space probe reaches a planet, parachutes open to let it slowly sink to the planet's surface. As the probe descends, it collects information about the planet's atmosphere.

The Huygen probe was designed to investigate the atmosphere and surface of Titan, one of the moons of Saturn.

PEOPLE IN SPACE

Conditions in space are very different from conditions on Earth. Without special protection, astronauts would only survive for a few seconds. Despite these problems there are plans for people to work on the Moon and to visit Mars.

In the past, astronauts have visited the Moon. More may do so in the future.

DANGERS IN SPACE

Humans need to breathe oxygen to stay alive. Oxygen is one of the gases in the Earth's atmosphere. In space there is no atmosphere, which means there is no oxygen to breathe.

In space, in full sunlight above the Earth, the temperature rises to 150°C. In the Earth's shade, the temperature may drop to −150°C. Humans cannot survive at these temperatures.

The Sun releases harmful X-rays and ultra-violet rays. On Earth, we are protected from these rays by the atmosphere. In space there is no atmosphere to protect the astronauts.

This astronaut is repairing the Hubble Space Telescope. His space-suit protects him from the dangers of space.

WEIGHTLESSNESS

When a spacecraft is high above the Earth, gravity pulls it around the planet instead of down to the surface. The orbiting spacecraft and everything inside it behave as if they did not have any weight. This condition is called weightlessness. Everything inside the spacecraft can float freely in the air.

This astronaut can float upside-down in the spacecraft easily. At mealtimes, his food can do the same thing.

SURVIVING IN SPACE

When people travel in space they have to be protected from the harmful conditions. The conditions in space are kept comfortable by life-support systems which provide oxygen, remove carbon dioxide and dampness, and prevent the air from becoming too hot. When the astronauts are outside the spacecraft, they wear space-suits which provide them with all the life-support systems they need.

Weightlessness makes the muscles and bones become weaker so astronauts have to exercise regularly to keep them strong.

GLOSSARY

AMMONIA – a chemical with a strong smell.

ASTEROID – a piece of rock which is in orbit around the Sun. Asteroids vary in size from the size of a grain of sand to 940 km across.

AXIS – the imaginary line around which a planet turns. The north and south poles of a planet are at either end of its axis.

BIG BANG – the explosion which occurred when the universe began.

BLACK HOLE – part of a collapsed star which has such a strong force of gravity that light cannot escape from it.

CANYON – a steep-sided, deep valley through which a river may flow.

CARBON DIOXIDE – the gas that we exhale.

COMET – a large lump of rock and ice in orbit around the Sun that produces two tails when it is near the Sun.

CONSTELLATION – a shape made in the sky by a group of stars in the Milky Way Galaxy.

CRATER – a hollow on the surface of a planet or a moon made by a rock falling on it from space.

EARTH – the third planet from the Sun. It has a diameter of 12,756 km. It rotates once in 24 hours and takes 365.25 days to orbit the Sun. The Earth has one moon.

EQUATOR – an imaginary line around the middle of the Earth. The equator divides the Northern Hemisphere and the Southern Hemisphere.

GRAVITY – a pulling force between two large objects or a large object and a small object in the universe. Gravity causes objects to fall to Earth and stops everything on Earth from floating off into space.

HELIUM – a type of gas.

HURRICANE – a storm in which a very strong wind blows.

HYDROGEN – a type of gas.

IRON – a type of metal. When iron gets damp some of the iron atoms combine with oxygen atoms to form iron oxide which is rust.

JUPITER – The fifth planet from the Sun. It has a diameter of 142,984 km and rotates once in nine hours fifty minutes. It takes 11.86 Earth years to orbit the Sun. Jupiter has 16 moons.

MARS – The fourth planet from the Sun. It has a diameter of 6,787 km. It rotates once in 24 hours 37 minutes and takes 687 Earth days to orbit the Sun. It has two moons.

MERCURY – the closest planet to the Sun. It has a diameter of 4,878 km. It rotates once every 58.6 Earth days and takes 88 Earth days to orbit the Sun. It has no moons.

METEOR – a small piece of rock from space which gets close enough to Earth to be pulled towards it. A meteor burns up in the Earth's atmosphere.

METEORITE – a large piece of rock from space which gets close enough to the Earth to be pulled towards it. A meteorite does not burn up in the atmosphere, but falls to the Earth's surface where it may make a crater.

METHANE – a type of gas.

NEBULA – a cloud of gas and dust in which stars may form.

NEPTUNE – The eighth planet from the Sun. It has a diameter of 49,528 km. It rotates once in 16 hours 7 minutes and takes 164.8 Earth years to orbit the Sun. It has eight moons.

OXYGEN – the gas humans need in order to breathe.

PLUTO – The ninth planet from the Sun. It rotates once on its axis in 6.375 Earth days. It takes 248.5 Earth years to orbit the Sun. It has one moon.

RADIO WAVES – waves of energy that can pass through space and the atmosphere and carry information.

ROCKET – a machine which burns fuel and produces a jet of hot gases. The force of the gas jet moving out of the back of the rocket is balanced by a pushing force which moves the rocket in the opposite direction.

SATURN – The sixth planet from the Sun. It has a diameter of 120,536 km. It rotates once in 10 hours 39 minutes and takes 29.46 Earth years to orbit the Sun. It has 18 moons.

TELESCOPE – a device which makes distant objects seem closer than they really are.

THERMOMETER – a piece of equipment that measures the temperature.

URANUS – The seventh planet from the Sun. It has a diameter of 51,118 km. It rotates once in 17 hours 14 minutes and takes 84.01 Earth years to orbit the Sun. It has 15 moons.

VENUS – The second planet from the Sun. It rotates once in 117 Earth days. It takes 225 Earth days to orbit the Sun. Venus has no moons.

VOLCANO – a mountain which has tube called a vent through which material from inside the planet escapes onto the planet's surface or into its atmosphere.

INDEX